D0571116

Bernice Hurst

for one
or two

simple and delicious easy-to-make recipes

p

This is a Parragon Publishing Book
This edition published in 2004

Parragon Publishing
Queen Street House
4 Queen Street
Bath BA1 1HE
United Kingdom

Copyright © Exclusive Editions 2002

All rights reserved. No part of this publication may be
reproduced, stored in a retrieval system, or transmitted, in any
form or by any means, electronic, mechanical, photocopying,
recording, or otherwise, without the prior permission of the
copyright holder.

ISBN: 1-40543-860-6

Printed in China

Produced by
THE BRIDGEWATER BOOK COMPANY LTD

Art Director Sarah Howerd
Editorial Director Fiona Biggs
Senior Editor Mark Truman
Photographer Simon Punter
Home Economist Ricky Turner

COVER
Photographer Mark Wood
Home Economist Pamela Gwyther

NOTES FOR THE READER

- This book uses both imperial and metric measurements. Follow the same units of measurement throughout; do not mix imperial and metric.

- All spoon measurements are level: teaspoons are assumed to be 5 ml, and tablespoons are assumed to be 15 ml.

- Unless otherwise stated, milk is assumed to be full fat, eggs are large, individual vegetables such as potatoes are medium, and pepper is freshly ground black pepper.

- Recipes using raw or very lightly cooked eggs should be avoided by infants, the elderly, pregnant women, convalescents, and anyone suffering from an illness.

- Optional ingredients, variations or serving suggestions have not been included in the calculations.
  The times given are an approximate guide only. Preparation times differ according to the techniques used by different people and the cooking times may also vary.

contents

introduction

Cooking for one or two provides an opportunity for experimentation and creativity without too much wastage. It enables you to try out new ingredients and recipes on a small scale so that you can decide what you do and don't like (in terms of ingredients, combinations, and method) and calculate how to make amendments or improvements next time. You have only yourself, and perhaps one other, to please.

If you believe that food is something to be enjoyed, and frequently shared, then cooking for one or two is the time to perfect your ideas and cooking skills.

The recipes in this book can easily be increased or decreased so that any one of them is suitable for one, two, or more if you decide to invite a few friends to dinner.

pan-braised chicken,
page 10

cured ham with glazed sautéed
pineapple, page 42

As with most cookbooks, this one has a selection of recipes that should not only make delicious dining but, hopefully, provide inspiration and give you the confidence to create your own dishes.

easy

Recipes are graded as follows:
1 spoon = easy;
2 spoons = very easy;
3 spoons = extremely easy.

serves 2

Recipes serve one or two people, as stated in each recipe. When dapting to make more or less, take care not to mix imperial and metric measurements.

10 minutes

Preparation time. Where chilling or marinating is involved, the time needed is shown separately: eg, 10 minutes + 30 minutes to chill.

30 minutes

Cooking time.

broiled lemon salmon,
page 60

quick macaroni salad,
page 76

When cooking poultry for one or two people, you can either select the cuts that you need or buy a whole bird, then cut it into portions, and prepare those portions separately in a number of different ways. Chicken, turkey, and duck all lend themselves well to recipes that are quick and easy or long and slow (but not necessarily difficult). The meat combines well with sweet ingredients, as in Broiled Chicken & Pineapple, and with hot spices, as in Spicy Bell Pepper Chicken or Broiled Mexican Chicken, while dishes, such as Crispy Crumb Turkey bring out the full flavor of the meat.

poultry

broiled chicken & pineapple

very easy   serves 1

5 minutes +   20 minutes
30 minutes
to marinate

ingredients

MARINADE
1 tbsp olive oil
juice of 1 lime

1 skinless, boneless chicken
  breast portion
2 pineapple slices
1 tbsp butter, melted

cooked snow peas, to serve

Combine the oil and lime juice in a glass dish. Place the chicken in the dish, stir well to coat in the marinade, cover with plastic wrap, and chill in the refrigerator for 30 minutes, turning once.

Remove the chicken from the refrigerator. Discard the marinade.

With the broiler at high, cook the chicken on the rack, skin side up, for 5 minutes, or until brown. Reduce the heat to medium and cook for 5 minutes more. Turn and cook for 10 minutes on the second side.

When you turn the chicken to cook on the second side, brush the pineapple slices with melted butter and place them on the broiler pan. Broil the pineapple for 5 minutes on each side so that it is piping hot and golden.

To serve, arrange the chicken on a serving dish and top with overlapping pineapple slices. Serve with snow peas.

pan-braised chicken

very easy   serves 2

10 minutes   60 minutes

ingredients

2 tbsp olive oil

2 chicken leg quarters

1 small onion, chopped roughly

4 tomatoes, diced

3 tbsp diced red bell pepper

1 small zucchini, sliced thinly
  or diced

8 white mushrooms, sliced thinly

1 garlic clove, crushed

 1 small fresh chili, seeded and diced
  or ½ tsp chili flakes (optional)

1 tsp dried oregano or basil

salt and pepper

scant 1 cup chicken stock

Heat the oil over high heat in a large skillet. Sauté the chicken for about 5 minutes, skin side down, until golden brown. Turn and brown the second side.

Add the onion, tomatoes, bell pepper, zucchini, mushrooms, garlic, and chili or chili flakes, if using. Sprinkle in the herbs and season to taste with salt and pepper. Mix well.

Pour in the stock, bring to a boil, then reduce the heat so that the liquid is just simmering. Cover the skillet and cook for 45 minutes, turning the chicken occasionally.

Transfer the chicken to a serving dish and keep it warm in a low oven. Increase the heat to high and boil the sauce hard so that it thickens and reduces. Spoon it over the chicken and serve.

crispy crumb turkey

very easy   serves 1

10 minutes   10 minutes

ingredients

1 large boned turkey breast fillet
1 heaping tbsp all-purpose flour
salt and pepper
1 egg, beaten

2 heaping tbsp fresh white
  bread crumbs
2 tbsp vegetable oil

Place the turkey fillet between 2 sheets of waxed paper and beat with a mallet or rolling pin to flatten.

Season the flour with salt and pepper. Remove the paper from the turkey and dredge the fillet in flour. Gently shake off any excess.

Dip the turkey in the egg and then in the crumbs, taking care that it is well coated.

Heat the oil over high heat in a shallow skillet. Fry the turkey for about 5 minutes, or until golden, then turn and continue frying until the second side is golden. Remove from the skillet and drain on paper towels before serving.

spicy bell pepper chicken

very easy   serves 2

10 minutes   15 minutes

2 boneless chicken breast portions

3 tbsp cornstarch

2 tbsp oil

1 green bell pepper, diced

3 garlic cloves, finely chopped

5 or 6 scallions, chopped

¼ tsp cayenne pepper

SAUCE

½ cup dark soy sauce

½ cup water

3 tbsp white wine vinegar

2 tsp sugar

Cut the chicken into bite-size pieces. Place them in a mixing bowl, sprinkle with cornstarch, and toss to coat.

To make the sauce, combine the soy sauce, water, vinegar, and sugar in a small bowl.

Heat the oil over high heat in a wok or pan large enough to hold the sauce and chicken. Stir-fry the chicken, bell pepper, and garlic for about 5 minutes, or until the meat is lightly browned.

Add the sauce mixture, reduce the heat, cover, and cook gently for about 5 minutes.

Stir in the scallions and cayenne pepper. Remove the lid from the pan and continue to cook over moderate heat for 3 more minutes to combine the flavors.

seared duck breast with orange honey glaze

very easy   serves 1

5 minutes   30 minutes

1 boneless duck breast

SAUCE
1 tbsp honey
½ tbsp orange juice
½ tsp soy sauce

Score the skin of the duck breast diagonally at 1 inch/2.5 cm intervals. Preheat the oven to 400°F/200°C.

Heat a heavy griddle until it is smoking. Place the duck on the griddle, skin side down, and cook over high heat for 5 minutes, or until starting to brown. Turn, reduce the heat, and cook over medium heat for 5 minutes more.

Transfer the duck to a roasting pan, skin side up, and put the pan into the oven for 15 minutes.

While the duck is cooking, combine the honey, orange juice, and soy sauce to make the sauce for glazing.

Remove the duck from the oven, pour the sauce over it, and return to the oven for a further 5 minutes.

Serve the duck breast whole or thinly sliced, cut at an angle.

belgian endive, orange & turkey salad

extremely easy

serves 2

10 minutes
+ 1 hour
to chill

ingredients

2 heads Belgian endive
2 oranges
scant ½ cup strips of cooked turkey

DRESSING
6 tbsp oil
3 tbsp orange juice
pinch of sugar
pinch of mustard powder
salt and pepper

Remove the outer leaves from the Belgian endive and slice them thinly widthwise. Peel the oranges and slice thinly against the grain, removing all the seeds.

Combine the Belgian endive and orange in a large mixing bowl.

To make the dressing, combine the oil, orange juice, sugar, mustard, salt, and pepper in a jar with a tight-fitting lid, then screw on the lid, and shake well. Pour the dressing over the Belgian endive and orange, toss well to blend, cover with plastic wrap, and chill for at least 1 hour.

Remove the salad from the refrigerator 10 minutes before serving. Toss once more, if desired, then arrange on attractive plates, and sprinkle the turkey strips on top.

broiled mexican chicken

very easy   serves 2

10 minutes
+ 30 minutes
to chill   15 minutes

ingredients

2 skinless, boneless chicken
  breast portions
juice of 1 lemon
2 tbsp olive oil
1 small onion, sliced thinly
1 small red bell pepper,
  seeded and sliced thinly
1 small green bell pepper, seeded and
  sliced thinly
1 tsp chili powder
½ tsp black pepper

SERVING SUGGESTIONS
sour cream
guacamole
refried beans
grated cheese
shredded lettuce
jalapeño chiles
salsa
tortillas, rice, or baked potato

Cut each chicken portion into 4 strips lengthwise. Place in a dish, sprinkle with lemon juice, mix, cover, and chill for 30 minutes.

Heat 1 tablespoonful of olive oil on high on a heavy griddle and toss on the onion and bell peppers. Cook over medium heat for 3 minutes, then sprinkle with chili powder, and mix well. Cook for 2 minutes more, then transfer to a warm serving dish.

Remove the chicken from the refrigerator and discard the lemon juice. Sprinkle with black pepper. Heat the remaining olive oil over high heat on the griddle and toss on the chicken. Cook, stirring frequently, for about 5 minutes.

Return the vegetables to the pan and cook for 3–4 minutes to combine the flavors.

Serve the chicken and vegetables immediately, accompanied by any or all of the serving suggestions listed above.

Many cuts of meat are ideal for those occasions when you are cooking for one and short of time. Most steaks, cutlets, and chops can be broiled or pan cooked, and, like Salisbury Steak or Pork in White Wine & Olive Sauce, will be ready in minutes. On the other hand, when you have more time to wait for your supper, there is little that is more comforting than tender, slow-cooked Veal & Tomato Stew, Lamb Curry, or gently cooked Paprika Pork. And when you have plenty of time for preparation, try the handmade Meatballs & Spaghetti like mama used to make.

meat

chili con carne

very easy   serves 2

10 minutes   60 minutes

ingredients

1 tbsp oil
1 small onion, chopped coarsely
1 or 2 garlic cloves, chopped coarsely
1 green bell pepper, seeded and diced
2 cups ground beef
1 heaping tsp chili powder
14 oz/400 g canned chopped tomatoes
½ tsp salt, optional
14 oz/400 g canned kidney beans,
  drained and rinsed

SERVING SUGGESTIONS
grated cheese
shredded lettuce and tomatoes
guacamole
jalapeño chiles
rice or tortillas

Heat the oil over low heat in a shallow skillet. Stir in the onion, garlic, and green bell pepper and cook gently for 5 minutes.

Add the beef and stir well. Turn up the heat to high and cook for 5 minutes, stirring occasionally. Spoon off any excess fat. Sprinkle in the chili powder and mix well. Continue cooking for 2–3 minutes. Stir in the tomatoes, reduce the heat, cover, and cook gently for at least 30 minutes. You may need to add more tomatoes or a little water or beef stock if it starts to dry out.

Check for seasoning and stir in the salt if needed. Add more chili powder to taste, but be careful not to overdo it. Add the drained kidney beans to the chili mixture 10–15 minutes before the end of the cooking time so that they heat through with the meat and spices.

Serve with any of the accompaniments listed above.

meatloaf

very easy   serves 2

10 minutes   45 minutes

ingredients

1 thick slice crustless white bread
water, to soak
3 cups ground beef, pork,
  or lamb
1 small egg
1 tbsp finely chopped onion
1 beef bouillon cube, crumbled
1 tsp dried herbs

salt and pepper

SERVING SUGGESTIONS
gravy or tomato or mushroom sauce
mashed potatoes
carrots or green vegetables

Preheat the oven to 350°F/180°C.

Put the bread into a small bowl and add enough water to soak. Let stand for
5 minutes, then drain, and squeeze well to get rid of all the water.

Combine the bread and all the other ingredients in a large bowl. Shape into a loaf,
then place on a cookie sheet or in an ovenproof dish. Put the meatloaf in the
oven and cook for 30–45 minutes, or until the juices run clear when it is pierced
with a toothpick.

Serve with your favorite sauce or gravy, mashed potatoes, and cooked carrots or a
green vegetable.

salisbury steak

very easy   serves 1

5 minutes   15 minutes

ingredients

1 tbsp vegetable oil
1 small onion, sliced thinly
4 white mushrooms, sliced thinly
1 cup ground beef

salt and pepper
¼ ciabatta
¼ cup red wine or beef stock

Heat the oil over high heat in a small skillet. Add the onion and mushrooms and cook quickly until soft. Push the vegetables to the side of the skillet.

Season the beef with salt and pepper, then shape into a round patty. Add to the skillet and cook until starting to brown, then carefully flip over, and cook the second side.

Slice the ciabatta through the middle, toast lightly, and arrange on a serving dish.

Remove the meat patty from the skillet and set it on the ciabatta.

Bring the onions and mushrooms back to the center of the skillet, pour in the wine, and heat until boiling. Continue boiling for 1 minute, or until slightly reduced, then remove from the heat, and spoon over the meat patty. Serve immediately.

veal & tomato stew

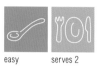

easy   serves 2

10 minutes   1¼ hours

ingredients

2 tbsp all-purpose flour
salt and pepper
2 tsp mixed dried herbs
12 oz/350 g stewing veal, cubed
2 tbsp olive oil
1 small red bell pepper,
    chopped coarsely

1 small green bell pepper,
    chopped coarsely
14 oz/400 g canned
    chopped tomatoes
¼ cup white wine

rice or fresh pasta, to serve

Combine the flour, salt, pepper, and herbs in a mixing bowl. Add the veal cubes
and toss to coat. Shake off any excess flour.

Preheat the oven to 325°F/160°C.

Heat the oil over high heat in a large skillet. Quickly cook the veal pieces, a few at
a time, until brown all over. Remove the meat from the skillet with a slotted spoon,
draining well, and transfer to a casserole.

When all the meat has been browned, add the bell peppers to the skillet, and stir
over high heat for 2 minutes. Remove with a slotted spoon and add to the
casserole. Pour in the tomatoes and wine, stir once, cover, transfer to the oven,
and bake for 1 hour, or until the meat is very tender.

Remove from the oven and spoon the veal, bell peppers, and sauce onto a bed rice
or fresh pasta.

italian sausages with bell peppers & potatoes

very easy   serves 2

10 minutes   20–30 minutes

ingredients

4 Italian sausages, sweet and/or spicy
1 small red bell pepper, seeded
   and cut into 8 pieces
1 small green bell pepper, seeded
   and cut into 8 pieces

2 unpeeled medium waxy potatoes,
   cut into 4 pieces
1 medium onion, sliced thickly
2 tbsp olive oil

Preheat the oven to 375°F/190°C.

Place the sausages in a large, shallow ovenproof dish.

Sprinkle the bell peppers, potatoes, and onion around the sausages.
Sprinkle with olive oil.

Cook the sausages and vegetables in the oven for 20–30 minutes,
turning occasionally.

Serve from the dish, while still hot.

pork in white wine & olive sauce

very easy   serves 1

5 minutes   25 minutes

ingredients

1 tsp olive oil

1 boneless pork steak

¼ tsp dried oregano

¼ tsp dried thyme

salt and pepper

2 tsp lemon juice

4 tbsp dry white wine

4 tbsp water

6 black olives

rice or fresh pasta, to serve

Sprinkle oil over the pork steak. Rub in the herbs and salt and pepper to season.

Heat a nonstick skillet and brown the pork quickly over high heat, turning once.

Pour in the lemon juice, wine, and water. Bring to a boil, then reduce the heat, cover, and simmer gently for 15 minutes.

Add the olives to the skillet and continue cooking for 5 minutes more to heat through.

Serve with rice or fresh pasta.

crunchy beef with hot citrus sauce

very easy   serves 2

5 minutes
+ 15
minutes to
marinate

10 minutes

MARINADE

1 tsp dark soy sauce

1 tsp fish sauce

1 garlic clove, crushed

oil, for deep-frying

8 oz/225 g steak, cut into thin strips

2 tbsp cornstarch

CITRUS SAUCE

6 tbsp brown sugar

1 tsp cornstarch

4 tbsp dark soy sauce

4 tbsp rice wine

grated rind and juice of 1 orange

SERVING SUGGESTIONS

broccoli or bok choy, stir-fried with garlic

spring rolls

Combine the soy sauce, fish sauce, and garlic in a mixing bowl. Add the strips of meat, stir to coat, cover, and chill 15 minutes.

Heat enough oil in a wok or large skillet to deep-fry the meat. Remove the meat, drain off the marinade, and toss the meat in cornstarch. Shake off any excess. Drop the strips of meat into the hot oil and cook quickly for 1–2 minutes, or until golden brown. Remove with a slotted spoon and drain on paper towels.

To make the sauce, combine the brown sugar and cornstarch in a small pan. Stir in the soy sauce, rice wine, and orange juice. Bring to a boil, then simmer gently for 2 minutes, stirring constantly.

Return the beef and 1 tablespoon of oil to the wok or skillet. Sprinkle in the orange rind. Stir quickly to reheat.

Transfer the beef to a serving dish and pour the sauce over it. Serve immediately with one or two of the other dishes suggested.

paprika pork

very easy   serves 2

10 minutes   1 hour

ingredients

3 tbsp all-purpose flour
1 tbsp paprika
pinch of salt
12 oz/350 g boneless pork
   steak, cubed
1 small onion, sliced thinly
14 oz/400 g canned
   chopped tomatoes

½ cup sour cream,
   to garnish

fresh egg noodles or potato pancakes, to
   serve

Preheat the oven to 350°F/180°C.

Combine the flour, paprika, and salt in a large mixing bowl. Add the pork and toss to coat.

Remove the meat from the flour, shaking off any excess, and place in a deep casserole. Arrange the onions on top and pour in the tomatoes.

Cover the casserole and cook in the oven for 1 hour, or until the meat is tender.

Remove the casserole from the oven and transfer the meat and sauce to a serving dish. Spoon the sour cream over the top.

Serve with egg noodles or potato pancakes.

beef with bell peppers & tomatoes

very easy   serves 1

5 minutes   10 minutes

2 tbsp all-purpose flour
salt and pepper
1 very thin Delmonico or sirloin steak
1 tbsp olive oil
1 tbsp sweet butter

SAUCE
½ small red bell pepper, diced
2 tomatoes, peeled and diced
¼ cup dry white wine
2 tbsp lemon juice

Season the flour with salt and pepper. Dredge the steak in the flour, shaking off any excess.

Heat the oil over high heat in a large skillet. When it is sizzling, add the butter, and cook until melted. Swirl the skillet around to combine the oil and butter.

Cook the steak in the skillet over high heat for 1–2 minutes depending on the thickness, then turn, and cook the other side for 1–2 minutes. The meat should not be too rare for this dish.

Transfer the cooked steak to a warm serving dish. Scrape the bottom of the skillet with a wooden spoon to incorporate any sediment that has stuck to the bottom.

Add the diced bell pepper and tomatoes to the skillet and mix well. Stir in the wine and lemon juice. Bring to a boil, reduce the heat, and simmer for 2 minutes. Pour over the steak and serve.

cured ham with glazed sautéed pineapple

very easy

serves 2

5 minutes   10 minutes

ingredients

1 thick cured ham steak
2 tsp brown sugar
½ tsp mustard powder
2 tbsp butter
2 slices of pineapple

TO SERVE
baked potato
green beans

Preheat a griddle or the broiler to medium and cook the ham steak for 5 minutes, turning once.

Combine the brown sugar and mustard in a small bowl.

Melt the butter in a small skillet, add the pineapple, and cook for 2 minutes to heat through, turning once. Sprinkle with the sugar and mustard and continue cooking over low heat until the sugar has melted and the pineapple is well glazed. Turn the pineapple once more so that both sides are coated with sauce.

Place the ham steak on a plate and arrange the pineapple, overlapping, on top. Spoon on some of the sweet pan juices.

Serve with a baked potato and green beans.

roast tomato & lamb packets

very easy   serves 1

10 minutes   45 minutes

ingredients

1 tbsp vegetable oil
1 large (or 2 small) lamb chop(s) or steak(s)
4 cherry tomatoes
1 garlic clove, crushed
2 tsp fresh torn oregano or chopped rosemary
salt and pepper

Preheat the oven to 325°F/160°C.

Heat the oil over high heat in a heavy skillet and brown the lamb chop(s) or steak(s) on both sides.

Cut a large square of aluminum foil. Drain the meat and place in the center of the foil. Arrange the tomatoes and garlic on top of the meat. Sprinkle with the torn oregano or chopped rosemary, salt, and pepper. Fold the foil to seal the packet and transfer to a cookie sheet.

Bake in the oven for 45 minutes, or until the meat is tender.

Open the packet carefully so that the steam can escape, then transfer the meat and tomatoes to a serving dish. Spoon on the juices from the meat.

lamb curry

easy   serves 2

10 minutes   1–2 hours

ingredients

2 tbsp oil or ghee

1 onion, chopped

1 garlic clove, chopped

½ inch/1 cm piece fresh ginger root,
  peeled and chopped

1 tsp paprika

½ tsp cayenne pepper

½ tsp ground cumin

½ tsp ground coriander

½ tsp garam masala

1 lb/450 g boneless lamb, cubed

3 small tomatoes

½ tsp salt

¼ cup plain yogurt

TO SERVE

rice or nan

mango chutney or pickle

Heat the oil or ghee in a shallow pan over medium heat. Add the onions and garlic and cook until browned.

Add the ginger and continue cooking, stirring constantly, for 2 minutes more. Add the other spices and mix well. Reduce the heat and cook gently for 3 minutes.

Stir the lamb into the spice mixture and cook over medium heat until the meat is sealed all over.

Peel and chop the tomatoes. Add to the meat with the salt and yogurt. Stir well to blend, bring to a boil, then reduce the heat, and simmer, covered, until the meat is tender. This will take 1–1½ hours depending on the size of the lamb cubes and the depth of the pan.

Turn the curry into a serving dish and offer rice, nan, chutney, or pickle as accompaniments

meatballs & spaghetti

easy   serves 2

10 minutes
+ 20 minutes
to make
tomato sauce

30 minutes

ingredients

1 thick slice crustless white bread

water, for soaking

1 quantity tomato sauce (see spicy baked
   pasta, page 78)

2 cups ground beef

1 egg

1 tsp chopped fresh parsley

1 tsp chopped fresh basil

1 garlic clove, finely chopped

½ tsp salt

6 oz/175 g dried spaghetti

freshly grated Parmesan cheese,
   to serve

Put the bread in a shallow dish and add water just to cover. After 5 minutes, drain, and squeeze the bread to remove all the liquid.

Heat the tomato sauce in a large pan over medium heat. Reduce the heat and simmer gently.

Mix the bread, beef, egg, herbs, garlic, and salt by hand in a large bowl. Roll small pieces of the meat mixture into balls. Drop the meatballs into the tomato sauce, cover the pan, and cook over medium heat for 30 minutes.

Meanwhile, cook the spaghetti in plenty of boiling water for 10 minutes, or until al dente. Drain, rinse, and drain again.

Turn the spaghetti into a large shallow serving bowl. Arrange the meatballs and sauce on top. Sprinkle 2 tablespoons of freshly grated Parmesan cheese over the top and serve more cheese in a bowl on the side.

Fish and shellfish are endlessly variable, delicious, and healthy. You can use fish to make anything from a light salad to a hearty soup. You can bake it, broil it, or fry it, and serve it plain or fancy, with a whole variety of sauces. The most important thing is that the basic ingredients must be fresh. Try simple, warming dishes such as Baked Flounder or go for the exotic in Thai Coconut Fish. Produce a sophisticated meal in minutes, such as Goujons with Garlic Mayonnaise or enjoy a cool summer classic, such as Salade Niçoise.

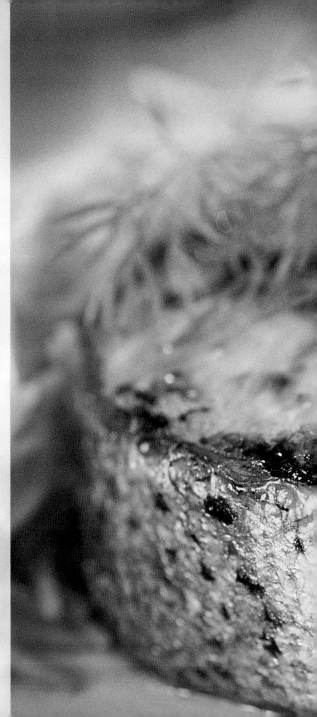

fish & shellfish

white fish chowder

very easy   serves 2

15 minutes   30 minutes

ingredients

4 tbsp butter

1 onion or leek, chopped roughly

½ green bell pepper, diced

1 large mealy potato, peeled
  and cubed

1¼ cups milk

salt and pepper

8 oz/225 g lb white fish fillets
  (cod, haddock or whiting)

generous 1 cup canned corn

2 tbsp chopped fresh parsley

crusty bread, to serve

Melt the butter over medium heat in a large, deep pan. Stir in the onion and bell pepper and cook until they just start to soften. Add the potato and mix well. Cook for 1 minute more.

Add the milk to the vegetables (except the corn), season well with salt and pepper, then increase the heat until the liquid is just about to boil. Reduce the heat slightly so that the milk is simmering, cover, and cook gently for 10 minutes, or until the potatoes are nearly soft.

Meanwhile, skin the fish and cut into ½ inch/1 cm strips. Add to the chowder and cook for 10 minutes more.

Stir in the corn and parsley. Cook for 5 minutes more, then serve with the crusty bread.

halibut with caramelized onions

very easy   serves 1

5 minutes   30 minutes

1 tbsp vegetable oil
½ small onion, sliced thinly
½ tsp balsamic vinegar
1 tbsp butter, melted
4 oz/115 g halibut fillet or steak

Heat the oil over medium heat in a large skillet. Add the onions, stir well, and reduce the heat. Cook for 15–20 minutes on a very low heat, stirring occasionally, until the onions are very soft and golden brown.

Add the vinegar to the onions and cook for 2 minutes more, stirring constantly to prevent them from sticking.

Brush melted butter over the fish.

Preheat the broiler or a griddle that goes on top of the stove. Sear the fish on high, then reduce the heat, and cook for about 10 minutes, turning once. Cooking time depends on the thickness of the fillet, but the fish should be firm and tender when done.

Remove the fish from the heat, place on a serving platter, and top with the caramelized onions.

crispy baked flounder

very easy   serves 2

10 minutes   25 minutes

4 oz/115 g flounder fillet
¼ cup butter, diced
1 tbsp lemon juice
salt and pepper

TOPPING
4 tbsp fresh white bread crumbs
1 tsp dried herbs (parsley, oregano,
   or thyme)
1 tsp mustard powder, optional
1 tbsp grated Cheddar cheese

Preheat the oven to 350°F/180°C.

Arrange the fish in a single layer in a shallow ovenproof dish.

Dot 2 tablespoons of butter over the fish. Sprinkle with lemon juice and season
with salt and pepper.

To make the topping, combine the bread crumbs with the herbs, mustard, and
cheese. Spoon the topping over the fish and dot with the remaining butter.

Put the dish in the oven and bake for 20 minutes. If necessary, place the dish
under the broiler for an extra 3–4 minutes to brown the topping before serving.

thai coconut fish

very easy   serves 2

10 minutes   15 minutes

ingredients

4 tbsp vegetable oil

1 shallot, chopped finely

½ inch/1 cm piece fresh ginger root or
   galangal, peeled and chopped finely

1 fresh chili, seeded and diced or
   ½ tsp dried chili flakes

6 sprigs fresh cilantro

½ cup coconut milk

8 oz/225 g white fish fillets

1 small leek, sliced thinly

Brown the shallot, ginger, and chili or chili flakes in 1 tablespoon of oil in a small skillet for 3–4 minutes. Turn into a blender or food processor. Add 2 sprigs of the cilantro, pour in the coconut milk, and process for 1 minute, or until smooth.

Meanwhile, half fill a large pan with water and bring to a boil.

Arrange the fish in a single layer in a glass dish that will rest on top of the pan without touching the water, then pour in the coconut sauce. Reduce the heat until the water is just simmering, then place the fish dish over the water to steam it. Cook for 10 minutes, or until the fish is firm and flakes easily with a fork.

Just before the fish is cooked, cook the leek in the remaining oil until crisp. Remove from the heat and drain on paper towels.

Transfer the fish to a serving dish, sprinkle with the leeks, and garnish with the remaining sprigs of cilantro.

broiled lemon salmon

extremely easy

serves 2

5 minutes

15 minutes

ingredients

4 oz/115 g salmon fillet or steak
juice of ½ lemon
1 tbsp butter, diced
salt and pepper

fresh parsley or dill, to garnish

Preheat the broiler to high.

Place the salmon fillet or steak on a rack over the broiler pan. Sprinkle lemon juice over the fish, dot with butter, and season with salt and pepper.

Cook for 10–15 minutes (or until the fish is firm and flakes when checked with a fork), turning once. Cooking time will vary depending on the thickness of the fillet.

Transfer to a serving dish and arrange sprigs of fresh herbs around the fish to garnish.

belgian endive crab salad

extremely easy

serves 2

20 minutes

8 oz/225 g white crab meat
2 tbsp ground sweet onion
2 tbsp finely chopped red bell pepper
1 tsp white wine vinegar
2 handfuls mixed salad greens
1 head of Belgian endive

DRESSING
¼ cup mayonnaise
2 tbsp tomato ketchup
pinch of cayenne pepper
1 tsp white wine vinegar
2 tbsp chopped fresh chives,
   to garnish

Flake the crab meat and mix in a large bowl with the onion and bell pepper. Sprinkle with vinegar, mix well, cover with plastic wrap, and chill in the refrigerator if not using immediately.

To make the dressing, combine the mayonnaise and ketchup. Season with cayenne pepper. Mix well. If the dressing is too thick, stir in 1 teaspoon vinegar.

Wash the salad greens and arrange in the bottom of a large serving dish or on individual plates. Trim the Belgian endive and slice thinly crosswise. Sprinkle it over the salad greens.

Remove the crab meat from the refrigerator 10 minutes before serving. Stir the crab meat mixture, then spoon it over the greens.

Drizzle the dressing over the crab meat. Sprinkle chives on top to garnish, then serve.

sweet & sour ginger fish

easy   serves 2

10 minutes   25 minutes

ingredients

2 large white fish fillets, skinned
1 egg, beaten
3 heaping tbsp all-purpose flour
oil for deep-frying
2 tbsp butter
1 green bell pepper, seeded and diced
5 scallions, thinly sliced

SAUCE
2 tsp cornstarch
1 tsp sugar
2 tsp wine vinegar
3 tsp sweet sherry
1¼ cups water
1 tbsp tomato paste
6 pieces preserved ginger, diced
1 tbsp ginger syrup

rice and salad, to serve

Cut the fish into large, bite-size pieces. Dip the pieces in the egg, then drain, and dredge in flour. Heat the oil and fry the fish pieces quickly for 3–4 minutes, or until they are golden brown. Drain on a dish lined with paper towels.

Melt the butter in a small skillet and cook the green bell pepper and scallions over medium heat for 5 minutes to soften.

Preheat the oven to 300°F/150°C.

To make the sauce, mix the cornstarch and sugar in a small bowl. Stirring constantly, add the vinegar and sherry, then gradually add the water and tomato paste. Finally, mix in the ginger pieces and syrup.

Arrange the fish in a shallow ovenproof dish. Pour the sauce over it and mix gently. Bake for 15 minutes.

Serve the fish with rice and mixed salad greens.

spaghetti with mussel sauce

very easy   serves 2

5 minutes   15 minutes

ingredients

1 lb/450 g live mussels
2 tbsp olive oil
8–10 fresh cherry tomatoes
¼ cup dry white wine
6 oz/175 g dried spaghetti or linguine
4 tbsp chopped fresh parsley

Remove the "beards" and wash the mussels in cold water to remove any sand, discarding any that are open.

Heat the olive oil over high heat in a large pan or flameproof casserole. Toss in the mussels, shake the pan, cover, and cook for 5 minutes, or until all the shells have opened.

Remove the lid from the pan, shake once more, add the tomatoes, and cook for 5 minutes more. Add the wine, reduce the heat, and continue cooking until the tomatoes are soft and the sauce thickens slightly.

Meanwhile, cook the spaghetti in a large pan of boiling salted water for 10 minutes, or until al dente. Drain in a colander, rinse under cold running water for a few seconds, then drain.

Add the spaghetti and parsley to the mussels mixture and stir well. Spoon into individual soup plates to serve.

baked trout with fennel

very easy   serves 1

5 minutes   20 minutes

ingredients

1 medium trout, cleaned but with
  the head on
1 large sprig of fresh fennel
1 tbsp butter, diced
1 tbsp lemon juice
salt and pepper

salad, to serve

Preheat the oven to 375°F/190°C.

Place the trout on a large square of aluminum foil and push the fennel inside the fish. Top the fish with diced butter and sprinkle with lemon juice. Season with salt and pepper.

Fold the foil around the fish to make a neat packet. Transfer the packet to a cookie sheet, place in the oven, and bake for 15–20 minutes. Open carefully so the steam escapes. The flesh should be firm and should flake easily with a fork. The eyes should now be white.

Transfer the packet to a cutting board. Unwrap the fish, remove the head and tail, and place the trout on a serving plate. Serve with a salad of your choice.

goujons with garlic mayonnaise

very easy   serves 2

10 minutes   5 minutes

6 tbsp mayonnaise
2 garlic cloves, peeled and crushed
2 large white fish fillets, skinned
1 egg, beaten
3 heaping tbsp all-purpose flour
oil for deep-frying

lemon wedges, to garnish

Combine the mayonnaise and garlic in a small dish. Cover with plastic wrap and chill in the refrigerator while you cook the fish.

Cut the fish into 1 inch/2.5 cm strips. Dip in the egg, then drain, and dredge in flour.

Meanwhile heat the oil. Fry the pieces of fish quickly in the oil until they are golden brown. This should take only 3–4 minutes. Remove the cooked fish from the oil and drain on a dish lined with paper towels.

Remove the garlic mayonnaise from the refrigerator and stir once. Set the drained fish on an attractive dish, garnish with lemon wedges, and serve with the mayonnaise on the side for dipping.

salade niçoise

very easy   serves 2

10 minutes   5 minutes
+ 2 hours
to chill

ingredients

2 fresh tuna steaks or
  7 oz/200 g canned tuna
1 tbsp vegetable oil
14 oz/400 g canned kidney
  or cannellini beans
4 cooked new potatoes, quartered
⅓ cup lightly cooked green beans, cut into
  ½ inch/1 cm pieces
2 tbsp finely chopped sweet onion
8 black olives

6 tbsp olive oil
3 tbsp red wine vinegar
½ tsp mustard powder or
  Dijon mustard
salt and pepper

2 hard-cooked eggs, quartered,
  to garnish

If using fresh tuna, brush on both sides with oil, then sear in a heavy griddle or skillet for 2 minutes on each side. Remove from the pan and cut into bite-size pieces. If using canned tuna, drain well, turn onto a plate, and flake with a fork.

Turn the canned beans into a strainer and rinse in cold water.

Combine the tuna, canned beans, potatoes, green beans, onion, and olives in a large mixing bowl.

Put the olive oil, vinegar, mustard, salt, and pepper in a jar with a tight-fitting lid. Screw on the lid and shake well, then pour the dressing over the tuna mixture and toss to combine. Cover with plastic wrap and chill for at least 2 hours. If you like, remove from the refrigerator about 30 minutes before serving.

To serve, mix the tuna and beans well to blend the flavors and textures. Turn into a serving dish and garnish with the egg pieces.

You don't have to be vegetarian to enjoy the occasional meat-free meal. All-in-one pasta dishes, such as Quick Macaroni Salad (cold) or Spicy Baked Pasta (hot), provide plenty of slow-release energy, while the Spanish Omelet makes an appetizing lunch or light supper. Quick and easy Eggplant & Goat Cheese Baguette or the unusual Pear & Blue Cheese Soufflé will make the most carnivorous among your friends and family think about becoming vegetarian.

vegetarian

quick macaroni salad

very easy   serves 2

10 minutes   15 minutes

ingredients

2 cups dried elbow or
  other small macaroni

1 scallion, sliced thinly

½ small green bell pepper, seeded
  and diced

½ small red bell pepper, seeded
  and diced

8–10 black olives, pitted
  and chopped

1 tsp chopped fresh parsley

1 tsp chopped fresh marjoram,
  oregano, or basil

2 tbsp white wine vinegar

6 tbsp olive oil

2 tbsp pine nuts

1 garlic clove, chopped finely

2 medium fresh tomatoes, peeled, seeded,
  and diced

Cook the macaroni in a large pan of boiling salted water for 8 minutes, or
until it is al dente. Drain, rinse in cold water, and drain again. Turn into a large
mixing bowl.

Add the scallion, green and red bell peppers, olives, and herbs. Mix well, then
sprinkle with vinegar, and mix again.

Heat the olive oil over high heat in a small skillet. Add the pine nuts and garlic,
reduce the heat to medium, and sauté gently for 3–4 minutes, or until they begin to
brown, taking care not to let them burn. Stir in the tomatoes and continue cooking
for 3 minutes more to warm them through.

Pour the tomatoes and pine nuts over the macaroni. Mix together well. Cool
slightly, but do not chill. Serve the macaroni salad at room temperature.

spicy baked pasta

very easy   serves 2

10 minutes   45 minutes

TOMATO SAUCE
14 oz/400 g canned
   chopped tomatoes
½ tsp dried oregano
½ tsp dried basil
½ tsp salt
1 small fresh chili, seeded
   and chopped finely or
   ½–1 tsp dried chili flakes

½ tsp garlic powder (optional)
pinch of fennel seeds (optional)
pinch of sugar (optional)

1½ cups dried penne, ziti, or other large
   macaroni
1 cup grated mozzarella cheese
2 tbsp freshly grated Parmesan cheese

To make the sauce, combine the tomatoes, herbs, salt, and fresh chili or chili flakes in a small pan. Add the garlic powder, fennel seeds, and sugar, if using. Bring to a boil, reduce the heat, and simmer gently for 15 minutes. Taste for seasoning and adjust if necessary. The sauce can be made in advance and reheated while the pasta is cooking.

Preheat the oven to 350°F/180°C.

Meanwhile, cook the pasta in a large pan of boiling salted water for 10 minutes, or until it is al dente. Drain, rinse with cold water, and drain again. Turn the pasta into a shallow ovenproof dish.

Remove the sauce from the heat and pour it over the pasta. Add the mozzarella and mix well. Sprinkle with Parmesan and bake in the oven for 30 minutes, or until the mozzarella is melted.

baked ravioli with tomato & cheese sauce

very easy   serves 2

5 minutes
+ 20 minutes
to make
tomato sauce

20 minutes

1 quantity tomato sauce (see spicy baked
    pasta, page 78)
8 oz/225 g fresh ravioli, tortellini, or other
    stuffed pasta
3 tbsp freshly grated Parmesan cheese

CHEESE SAUCE
4 tbsp butter
2 tbsp all-purpose flour
½ cup milk
½ cup grated Cheddar cheese
salt and pepper

Prepare or reheat the tomato sauce (see page 78). Spread it in the bottom of a large, shallow ovenproof dish.

Preheat the oven to 350°F/180°C.

Meanwhile, cook the pasta in a large pan of boiling salted water for 3 minutes. Drain, rinse with cold water, and drain again. Turn into the dish containing the tomato sauce.

Make the cheese sauce by melting the butter in a medium pan over low heat. Stir in the flour until it has all been absorbed. Gradually add the milk, stirring constantly, and cook over medium heat, still stirring, to thicken. Add the cheese and continue cooking until it has melted. Season to taste.

Spoon the cheese sauce over the pasta in its ovenproof dish. Sprinkle with Parmesan. Bake for 5–10 minutes, or until the top is golden and the sauce is bubbling. Serve from the dish.

spanish omelet

very easy   serves 1

10 minutes   10 minutes

ingredients

2 tbsp butter

1 tbsp chopped onion

1 tbsp chopped green bell pepper

4 white mushrooms, diced

1 small cooked waxy potato, diced

2 large eggs

1 tbsp milk

salt and pepper

2 tbsp grated Cheddar cheese

Melt the butter over medium heat in a large skillet.

Add the onion, bell pepper, and mushrooms. Stir well to coat in butter and cook for about 3–4 minutes, or until soft. Mix in the potato and cook for 2 minutes more to heat through.

Beat the eggs with the milk, salt, and pepper. Pour over the vegetables in the skillet and reduce the heat to low. Cook the egg mixture, occasionally lifting the edges and tilting the skillet to let the liquid run to the outside.

Preheat the broiler to high.

When the eggs are mostly set, with only a small wet patch in the middle, sprinkle the cheese on top. Place the whole skillet under the broiler and cook for 2 minutes, or until the cheese has melted and is golden brown. Serve immediately.

penne with hot pepper broccoli

very easy   serves 2

5 minutes   15 minutes

ingredients

1½ cups dried penne, ziti or other large
   macaroni
1 small head fresh broccoli,
   cut into florets
4 tbsp olive oil
2 garlic cloves, slivered

1 small fresh chili, seeded and
   cut into thin strips, or 1 tsp dried chili
   flakes

TO SERVE
1 tbsp chopped fresh basil
freshly grated Parmesan cheese

Cook the penne in a large pan of boiling salted water for 10 minutes, or until it is al dente. Drain, rinse with cold water, and drain again. Return to the pan.

Meanwhile, cook the broccoli in a large pan of boiling salted water for 6–8 minutes. It should be only just tender. Remove from the heat, drain, rinse with cold water, and drain again.

Heat the oil in a large skillet over high heat until it is sizzling. Add the garlic and fresh chili or chili flakes and cook for 1 minute. Add the broccoli and mix well. Reduce the heat to medium and cook for 2 minutes more to heat through.

Pour the broccoli and garlic mixture over the penne and mix well. Turn into a large serving dish and sprinkle with basil and cheese.

pear & blue cheese soufflé

easy   serves 2

10 minutes   40 minutes

ingredients

scant ½ cup water
¼ cup sugar
1 small pear, peeled and quartered
1 tbsp butter
1 tbsp all-purpose flour
⅔ cup milk

½ cup crumbled blue cheese,
    such as Danish Blue
1 egg yolk
2 egg whites

Heat the water and sugar in a pan, stirring until dissolved. Increase the heat, boil vigorously for 5 minutes, reduce to a simmer, add the pear, and poach gently for 10 minutes. Drain and dice the pear and put the pieces in 2 buttered ramekins.

Melt the butter in a small pan, add the flour, and stir until it is absorbed. Gradually add the milk and cook, still stirring, until thick. Add the blue cheese and stir until melted. Remove the sauce from the heat and stir in the egg yolk.

Preheat the oven to 350°F/180°C.

Whisk the egg whites until they are stiff but not dry. Gently fold 2 tablespoons of egg white into the sauce to loosen the mixture. Fold the remaining egg whites gently into the sauce. Spoon into the ramekins and place them on a cookie sheet.

Put the cookie sheet in the oven and bake for 15 minutes, or until well risen. Serve immediately.

eggplant & goat cheese baguette

extremely easy   serves 2

10 minutes   20 minutes

ingredients

1 small eggplant
2 tbsp olive oil
1 tsp coarse sea salt
1 medium baguette or ciabatta
½ cup crumbled goat cheese
2 tbsp chopped fresh parsley or cilantro

Preheat the oven to 325°F/160°C.

Trim the eggplant and cut lengthwise into thin slices. Arrange in a single layer in a shallow ovenproof dish. Sprinkle with olive oil and sea salt. Bake for 15–20 minutes, or until very tender.

Cut the baguette into 2 pieces, each about 6 inches/15 cm long. Cut each piece in half lengthwise.

Place a layer of eggplant on the bottom piece of bread. Top with goat cheese and herbs. Press the top layer of bread down gently on the sandwich and serve while the eggplant is still warm.

eggs florentine

very easy   serves 1

5 minutes
+ 10 minutes
to make the
cheese sauce

20 minutes

ingredients

1 cup cooked spinach, chopped roughly
2 extra large eggs
salt and pepper
½ quantity cheese sauce (see baked ravioli
   with tomato & cheese sauce, page 80)
freshly grated Parmesan cheese, for sprinkling

Squeeze the spinach well to get rid of all the liquid.

Butter a shallow ovenproof dish and place the spinach in an even layer over the bottom.

Preheat the oven to 375°F/190°C.

Break the eggs onto the spinach. Season with salt and pepper.

Spoon the cheese sauce over the eggs, taking care not to break the yolks. Make sure the sauce covers the entire egg and spinach base. Sprinkle the top with Parmesan cheese.

Put the dish on a cookie sheet, place in the oven, and bake for 15–20 minutes. Serve immediately.

stuffed eggplant

very easy   serves 2

10–15 minutes   1–1½ hours

ingredients

1 lb/450 g onions, sliced thinly
3 garlic cloves, sliced thinly
⅔ cup olive oil
14 oz/400 g canned
    chopped tomatoes
pinch of sugar

1 tsp salt
4 tbsp chopped fresh parsley
1 large eggplant
juice of 1 lemon
2 tsp dried oregano

Cook the onions and garlic in ½ cup of olive oil in a large skillet, until soft but not brown. Add the tomatoes, raise the heat until the mixture boils, then reduce the heat, and simmer for 5 minutes. Season with sugar, salt, and parsley.

Preheat the oven to 325°F/160°C.

Cut the eggplant in half lengthwise and place, cut side up, in a large ovenproof dish. Spoon the onion and tomato over it. Sprinkle with lemon juice and oregano, then pour in the remaining olive oil. Add enough water to come to the top of the eggplant and topping. Cover and bake for 1–1½ hours, testing every half hour, pressing down or adding more water if necessary.

Remove the cooked dish from the oven and transfer the eggplant to a serving dish to eat hot. Alternatively, let cool in the covered dish until completely cold.

basic pizza dough & pizza topping

easy   serves 2

1¼ hours   10–20
+ 20 minutes   minutes
to make the
tomato sauce

ingredients

2 cups white bread flour, plus extra for
 kneading
1 tsp active dry yeast
1 tsp salt
2 tbsp olive oil
1 –1 ½ cups warm water

TOPPING
4 tbsp olive oil
1 large onion, sliced thinly

6 white mushrooms,
 sliced thinly
½ small green bell pepper, sliced thinly
1 quantity tomato sauce (see spicy
 baked pasta, page 78)
2 oz/55 g mozzarella cheese,
 sliced thickly
2 tbsp freshly grated Parmesan cheese

crisp salad, to serve

Combine the flour, yeast, and salt in a mixing bowl. Drizzle in 1 tablespoon of olive oil. Make a well in the center and pour in the water. Mix to a firm dough, shape into a ball, turn onto a floured surface, and knead until it is no longer sticky. Grease the bowl with the remaining oil. Put the dough in the bowl, turn to coat with oil, cover with a dish towel, and let rise for 1 hour.

When the dough has doubled in size, punch it down to release the excess air, then knead until smooth. Divide in half and roll into 2 thin rounds. Place on a pizza pan or cookie sheet.

For the topping, soften the vegetables for 5 minutes in the olive oil. Spread tomato sauce over the pizza base, but do not go right to the edge. Top with the vegetables and mozzarella cheese. Spoon over more tomato sauce, then sprinkle with Parmesan. Bake for 10 minutes at 425°F/220°C, or until the base is crisp and the cheese has melted. Serve with a crisp salad.

index